NO ONE IS ON THE LINE

THE POETRY OF MOHSEN MOHAMED

Translated from the Arabic by Sherine Elbanhawy

CHAPEL HILL
2023

First Edition

Printed in the United States of America
Cover and book design by Maxine Mills

"On the Bursh After Dinner" and "The Light Isn't Surrounded by Guards" first appeared in *ARABLIT & ARABLIT QUARTERLY* www.arabit.org., in 2021. Reprinted with kind permission.

ISBN 978-1-942281-30-6

Egret is an imprint of Laertes Press, Incorporated | www.laertesbooks.org

INTRODUCTION

Egypt's long history and its multiple political, economic, and geographical influences have imbued Egyptians with a certain adaptability. This is reflected in our language, which has an Arabic base but has absorbed vocabulary from so many other languages over the centuries such as Ancient Egyptian, Coptic, Greek, Italian, Turkish, Farsi, French, and English. The language we speak today, Egyptian Colloquial Arabic[1] (ECA, *'amiyya)*, continues to evolve every day. It constantly melds phrases and assimilates idioms from other languages. We grow up speaking 'amiyya but learn classical Arabic (formal/ standard, fusha) in school. This is the language we hear on the news and memorize in the Quran, but it is our beloved *'amiyya* that is the language of creativity and artistic and emotional expression. Its ubiquity in song, on screen, and in literature allowed Egyptian culture to propagate throughout the Arab world making ECA the most easily understood Arabic dialect and underscoring what is often referred to as Egypt's soft power.

ECA is also very political because of its populism. Since the 19th century, its poetry has been a reflection of the street's discontent, becoming an integral part of

1. 'Amiyya which comes from 'ammah meaning the masses, the language of the masses.

resistance movements. Elliott Colla reminds us in his article, *The Poetry of Revolt*, that when Egyptians rose against British colonialism (1919), poets like Bayram al-Tunisi and Badi' Khayri provided the soundtrack for anti-colonial dissent. After the fall of Egypt's monarchy in 1952, it was the poets "Salah Jahin and Fuad Haddad who fed the nationalist fervour" (Shaaban, 11). During the labor and student protests of the 1970s and 1980s, the poet Ahmed Fuad Negm electrified the masses and "played the leading role as lyricist of militant opposition to the regime of Egypt" (Colla).

The poetry of revolution profoundly impacted the country's cultural and artistic fabric; it was then no surprise that during the 2011 Egyptian Revolution, the chants and poems of Ahmed Fuad Negm, Salah Jahin, Fuad Haddad, and Abdel Rahman el-Abnoudi resurfaced and filled the streets. Their genre of Egyptian colloquial poetry "relies not only on a deep level of engagement with contemporary politics, but also on invective, wordplay, and folk idioms, or what is otherwise known as 'the language of the street'" (Shaaban, 10). Egyptians reclaimed the streets, their voices, and their cultural heritage during the Revolution. This is why the work of contemporary poets such as Tamim Barghouti became a means of political protest and social commentary, addressing themes such as corruption, poverty, and the daily struggles against injustice. There continues to be a solid literary-political tradition of Egyptian colloquial poetry that inspires new generations of poets who have added to it in their own ways, invigorating the genre and redefining it. Mohsen Mohamed is one of these poets.

Mohsen's poetry is very much ingrained in the tradition of poetry as a voice of resistance; his specificity to the Egyptian incarceration experience speaks to the broad themes of injustice, the harshness and the inhumanity of his time in prison, the friendships, and the community that the closeness of prison creates.

Mohsen and I met by chance at a workshop at the Cairo Institute of Liberal Arts Studies (CILAS) conducted by one of my friends, Mina Ibrahim. His poetic voice immediately resonated with me, and I asked if he had ever considered translation. At the time, there was no publishing promise or anything, just a craving on my part to be drawn into his world and the beautiful rhythmic flow of his Egyptian vernacular poetry.

Throughout the pandemic, I worked on this translation; I put my own work aside, feeling the need to give voice to Mohsen's words at that distinct point in history. At a time when everyone was complaining about the restrictions of being locked in within the comfort of their homes and surrounded by family, his experience and that of his fellow inmates was especially poignant. My mind constantly returned to the many unjustly incarcerated in Egypt and how their lives had been upended without due process. As the pandemic dragged on and the situation worsened on the outside, conditions in prison deteriorated even more given the lack of healthcare, hygiene, and sanitation.

Mohsen's ability to convey his deep sense of loneliness mirrored the feelings of many across the world and echoed vociferously on social media. However, his prison is a beast with a life of its own, a creature that devours and consumes. He is constantly surrounded, but isolated; his poems are a retreat into self, a journey of reflection and profound solitude. The title, *No One Is On The Line*, reflects this enveloping sense of disconnectedness. Even after his release, Mohsen's recollections show how the pain of prison and the feeling of isolation persist after incarceration ends, fed by the memories of friends and encounters imprinted on the soul.

The translation of Mohsen Mohamed's work has been a difficult and intimate journey. A decade after the Egyptian Revolution, it brings up many questions: Who pays the price of political activism? What kind of future do we have with so many unjustly incarcerated? What does it mean to silence and be silenced? How are we implicated through our silence? What does resistance mean? How can we as individuals work towards abolishing the inhumanity of mass incarceration?

Translating Egyptian colloquial poetry is difficult not only because of the complexity of Arabic grammar and syntax but also because of the need for conciseness and precision. There is a constant struggle to be true to the beauty and lyricism of the original, which is incredibly difficult to convey in English. I followed Spivak's advice that "the translator must surrender to the text. She must solicit the text to show the limits of its language because that rhetorical aspect will point at the silence of the absolute fraying of language that the text wards off, in its special manner. (…) translation is the most intimate act of reading" (Spivak, 400).

I have been sharing messages and voice notes with Mohsen throughout the process, for clarification, insight, and background on the poems to ensure no part of the meaning is lost. One of the results of this exchange was that our friendship also grew. We exchanged views of other literary works that inspire us, revealed dreams for the future, and shared moments of joy.

My commitment to conveying the precise meaning of each poem was not without its challenges. Mohsen infuses everything from Quranic references and Egyptian proverbs and idioms to prison language and culture into his work. I chose to add footnotes for context and to explain certain insinuations that may not be apparent to the reader unfamiliar with the background. It is important not only to understand his cultural references, but also his manipulation of religious discourse; his careful subversion of religious rhetoric and play upon the meaning of recognizable Qur'anic verses make the very familiar unexpected and illustrate how he pushes against dominant traditional understandings.

There are several choices I made together with Mohsen during the translation process. With his approval, we abandoned the punctuation conventions imposed by the publisher of the Arabic version for a more modern rendition in line with contemporary poetry. We also modified the line breaks where necessary to make rhythmic sense in English and chose to use less formal American English to help replicate the musicality Mohsen excels at with his choice of ECA over formal standard Arabic. I also frequently made use of alliteration to recreate much of the playfulness, allusion, and pathos Mohsen achieves in his description of the details of prison life.

My final choice reflects another of Spivak's concepts, which posits that as a translator, I do not have the responsibility to domesticate all the imagery and that I can invite the reader "to sit with the discomfort of not immediately or fully understanding and thus recognizing oneself as an outsider to the ritual. Translation thus begins with bringing the viewer as close as possible to the original, instead of bringing the ritual performance more palatable to the viewers' standpoint, thereby reducing it to a cliché or to the least common denominator" (Bala, 6).

I hope that my translation brings home the most authentic possible version of Mohsen's profound work, and I invite readers to move past their discomfort and reach out and learn more about the critical issues he presents.

For all the strength of unjust leaders across the world, and no matter how much wealth, military might or complete control they have, there is one thing that holds true: they fear words.

#FreeAlaa #FreeThemAll

—Sherine Elbanhawy

Abdel Nasser, Tahia. "Revolutionary Poetics and Translation." *Translating Dissent: Voices from and with the Egyptian Revolution,* Routledge, 2016, pp. 107–22.

Bala, Sruti. "Necessary Misapplications: the Work of Translation in Performance in an Era of Global Asymmetries," *South African Theatre Journal*, 33:1, 5-13, 2020. DOI: 10.1080/10137548.2020.1760126

Colla, Elliott. "The Poetry of Revolt." *Jadaliyya, Jadaliyya*, 31 Jan. 2011, https://www.jadaliyya.com/Details/23638/The-Poetry-of-Revolt.

Fahmy, Ziad. *Ordinary Egyptians: Creating the Modern Nation through Popular Culture*. Stanford University Press, 2011.

Shaaban, Salma Aly Khamis Mohamed. "Triple Bind: Iman Bakri's Vernacular Satirical Poetry as a Challenge to Dominant Language Ideologies." School of Languages, Cultures and Linguistics at the University of London's School of Oriental and African Studies (SOAS), 2019.

Spivak, Gayatri Chakravorty. "Translating into English." *Nation, Language, and the Ethics of Translation*, edited by Sandra Bermann and Michael Wood, Princeton: Princeton University Press, 2005, pp. 93-110. https://doi.org/10.1515/9781400826681.93

A PREFACE FROM MOHSEN MOHAMED

In the first week of my incarceration following my arrest at a student demonstration at Mansoura University in 2014, the first poem I tried to write almost got me into trouble. I was completely absorbed, hunched over my piece of paper and oblivious to my surroundings. Everyone noticed when the administrative officer came into the hall except me. Silence fell, but I was engrossed. I only realized how close the officer was when the guy sitting next to me gave me a nudge. I was caught red-handed and quickly tried to fold the paper, at a loss where to hide it. The poem and the officer had arrived at the same time, as if to crystallize my feelings, both of fear and of detachment.

The incident passed peacefully, but it was like a wake-up call for me. To remain safe while in detention, I realized I would need to use coded language whether I was writing a poem or even a just letter to my mother.

I devised a simple system, inserting extra letters to make my words illegible. I would add the letter "m" at the beginning of each word, a "d" and a "y" before the last letter. For example, I turned the word "aref" into "maredyf" and "nazl" into "mnazdyl." The new language was incomprehensible without an interpreter who would allow it to reappear and express itself without fear.

I remember moments when I would hide inside a word, a phrase, or a verse from a poem by Mahmoud Darwish. I would be in the middle of the crowd, yet I could carve out a space for myself and detach from my surroundings. My body would be crumpled in the corner, but I was floating above the space together with Darwish, both of us repeating, "I am my language."

I became obsessed with Fuad Haddad's poetry. His words always accompanied me in the prison hallways over the years. I wished I had a bedroom where I could hang his picture above my bed. Instead, I memorized his poems, imagined them on the walls of my cell, repeated them endlessly, everywhere.

I finally received a bed of my own when I was promoted to the status of long-timer. I used to lie there, humming the poems, counting the syllables on my fingers. I must have looked like a madman, sitting in the dark, moving my fingers, and whispering incomprehensible words to myself throughout the night. One of the people who observed my ritual later confessed that he suspected prison had made me lose my mind.

Poetry—both reading and writing it—provided a way for me to tune out my surroundings. This state of detachment may only have been temporary, but it was always available to me. Poetry in prison is like dreaming; it's an alternative space to live, experience, and see the world.

As the months passed, poetry became my measure of time. The details of my life were captured in the poems I wrote as I moved from one cell to the next. An hour became the number of poems I wrote as I glanced behind me at the cell I was leaving.

Once, I wrote a verse of poetry on my arm while in the prison transport van because there was no paper. In some solitary confinement cells, I had neither paper nor pen, the darkness so complete that I could barely see my body. There, I breathed the words of my most intimate and most crude poem. I still know it by heart, and it is the one that I hold dearest. I never published it or even wrote it down, but it lives, engraved on the walls of my memory.

My first attempts at poetry had begun two years before I was arrested, when I was nineteen years old and was just taking pictures of a female student being beaten up at a university protest that I hadn't even taken part in. First, I took pictures, then I tried to interfere and defend her. That's what got me arrested.

I spent five years in a world governed by arbitrary norms, a system indifferent to the humanity of its inmates. The prisoners' profound interest in poetry was, in my opinion, a way for them to somehow restore some dignity to their lives and preserve the meaning and value of their bodies and destinies.

We were all obsessed with poetry, almost as much as we were with the idea of an unconditional release from prison. We transformed the cell into a cultural salon, exchanging poems and songs and attending lessons on language and poetry given by detained university professors.

The convicted felons were known for a type of free verse known as "From the Ward." In the silence of the night, the inmates would start to recite from behind the bars of their cells, always beginning with a fixed or standard line, "Everyone in this ward, listen up! Even the iron bars, listen up!" and then they would use the numbers from one to ten to build a poetic framework of their personal stories within the prison walls, their life of crime, and their yearning for release.

This type of poetry is exclusive to the locality of prison as its title implies. I believe that this unique and relatively established part of prison culture deserves to be studied, in the hope that it will find its way beyond the prison walls and perhaps take its place among other genres of poetry.

The poems in this collection share an intimate relationship with the prisoners, each one born and bred within the world of the incarcerated. As soon as I finished writing, my fellow inmates were the first to hear my pieces whenever there was a chance.

My purpose in writing these poems was to attempt to live a normal, spontaneous life, to share experiences with the comrades who were part of my life for years. It makes me immensely happy when I encounter a stranger or a former prisoner who quotes or recites a verse of the prison poems to me.

There is considerable movement of prisoners between prisons. This has many purposes, such as sitting for exams, and creates a vital network of communication between prisoners in different prisons and cities. I was once transferred to the Shebin al-Kom prison for a week and was astonished to find that some of my poems had preceded me.

Prison made me appreciate what was real. That's why it was never surprising to see me in my cell spending all my time reading or writing a poem the night before my university exams.

Finally, after the collection was published and released in Cairo, I had the opportunity to meet the translator and beautiful human being Sherine Elbanhawy over Zoom to discuss the possibility of translation. I found that I could finally make fun of my old fears that the prison transport van would fall into the Nile, and all my poems, written on paper, would dissolve in the water and be lost forever.

Thank you, Sherine, for our friendship, for this beautiful translation and for contributing to the life journey of these living beings . . .

TIME

In
at twenty
out
at twenty.

You ask,
"But
how many
years inside?"
Sigh—
"A lifetime confined."

In
at twenty
out
at twenty,
with
new notions of time.

ON THE ROAD

On this road in a blue uniform
I walked,
and on that road over there,
I was taken away.
On that road,
I laughed till I wept,
tenderness tasered away – dazed.

On that road,
I saw home,
like an instant caught on tape,
stuck on repeat,
as you run on asphalt.

The transport van
a cancer,
gnawing at the roads.
The city is a body,
drowned in sleep,

that suddenly contains
a prison on wheels.
If you happen to ride in it,
you'll see
all walks of life
walking about.
An incredible feat in itself,
if only you knew.[1]

Or if you once happen to ride
the international highway to Natroun,[2]
you'll take in the sights,
the people, listen to the sounds,
all the while, you are the alien—
voiceless, invisible,
screaming like the dead.

---

1. From the Quran verse 56:76: "and this, if only you knew, is indeed a great oath"— seeing things is of great consequence especially while going through forced disappearance.

2. A reference to Natroun prison, located in Wadi El Natroun, which is a valley with several alkaline lakes, natron-rich salt deposits (used historically in mummification), salt marshes, and freshwater marshes.

But no one will hear you
from now till doomsday.

If you spot your home through the wire mesh,
look away.

Your eye is no more than a memory,
like an instant caught on tape,
stuck on repeat,
as you run on asphalt.

On this road in a blue uniform,
I walked,
and on that road over there,
I was taken away.

Roads like memories are hazy.
In seconds,
they shape things that you forgot,
they startle
with something memory erased.

Me and my feelings
battered each other
when I recognized from the yard,
the home of my loved ones,
on a road
known to me only by its smell,
my hands cuffed behind me,
my eyes blindfolded.

On this road
I went,
on this road
I came.
On this road
I dreamt and yearned,
and so often on this road
I circled,
but never ever in the end
did I arrive.

On this road,

now,

I walk alone.

I call out in regret:

"If only our friends could stand with me

here on the asphalt."

KHALIFA POLICE STATION

Nightmares lie beneath
the night at the Khalifa,
and in the cells
day passes like night.

A night in lockup
is lost,
cosmic nights
perish
in confusion.

An hour of strangeness:
All the earth is Yours, God,
except this place underground,
where people
sleeping huddled
drown,
layer upon layer,
their bodies stacked together in rows.

The criminal world
is odd and wonderful,
full of yarns beyond belief:

Saeed Mosoghar,[3]
the safe cracker
his slender fingers no sooner touch
the dial, than it cracks.

The pickpocket
with shrewd eyes
and dark, stolen lashes.[4]

Shahat Alata,[5]
who steals from thieves,

---

3. All the names in the poem also characterize the individuals. It provides a levity and sarcasm that is lost in the translation. Mosoghar means locks.

4. A play on Egyptian proverb "Yessrak El-kohl min El-'Ain," someone is so deft that he could easily steal the kohl from a woman's eyelids.

5. Similar to footnote 5, Shahat Alata means the arrogant peddler.

Abdoh Medina,
the counterfeiter,

and Sayed Sefina,
who smuggles
packages so plump
they clog a rectum.

A drug-cooker in El-Hadayek
and a dealer in Rawd Al-Faraj,
another taken in for embezzlement,
well-connected and prominent.

My uncle Bilal, reported by his grandson,
sent down for bad checks,
complains of rheumatism gnawing away
at his joints.
In the heart of the nights,
his tattoo of a bride
grows to fill his arms
and enflame cold chains.

Salama El-Gareeb,[6] who
down-at-the-heel[7] traverses the world,
knows all the cities and streets,
the alleys, the walkways.
He reads facial expressions
in darkest night.
At a glance can tell
who is free or turning tricks
or passing time.
That one is sober, that one is drunk,
and that one is unlike any other.
Salama El-Ghareeb, so homesick
he strikes out at the horizon.
Whatever he comes across,
however remote and exotic,
puts him in mind of family,

---

6. El-Ghareeb means the stranger.

7. Kaa'b dayer means to wear out your heel. It's a saying that emanated from the police needing to take the accused through all the other police offices in the various governorates to ensure they weren't wanted for other crimes. This process took weeks, and sometimes up to a month, before the centralization and computerization of criminal records.

the homestead, villages,
or crops in the field.

Chika El-Mothaqaf,[8]
chivalrous and well-bred,
says in alliteration,
you chime in my chest and in me,[9]
my loyal chums.
I have friends of caliber
I can call on
and girlfriends I never transgressed with
except one who compelled me by necessity,[10]
just a one-off thing
but a happening I had need of.

---

8. El-Mothaqaf means the cultured/learned/literate.

9. "And in me" in Arabic (wafi) is homonymous with loyal (wafi).

10. A Quranic reference to Surah Al-Baqarah Ayat [2:173] "He has only forbidden you 'to eat' carrion, blood, swine and what is slaughtered in the name of any other than Allah. But if someone is compelled by necessity—neither driven by desire nor exceeding immediate need—they will not be sinful. Surely Allah is All-Forgiving, Most Merciful."

How astonishing
the criminal world,
reverting to the primitive,
resilient,
sleeping in rows,
sleeping upright.
How astonishing
humanity's lesson:
that people can only be made plain
under the harshest
conditions.

TRAVELING IN HANDCUFFS

Destitute,
shackled in the belly of a box.
Despite the band of metal
wrapped around each wrist,
I hold
my unknown comrade's hand.
Our relationship is most definitely strong,
sanctioned by iron restraints.

Carrying bags
stuffed with clothes and qualms
and covers for the tile floors
when they give us their hugs.
Crying and wailing,
carrying bags
stuffed with hell and damnation,
shackled together,
hand in hand.

In moving boxes like caves,
why is more than my wrist restrained?
Destitute, shackled,
carrying all our belongings
in a bag.

VOID

In the dark, his groans are captive,
the sons of bitches torturing the lions in a circus.
Tenacity grows in the void, and the weeping ceases.
The weeping abruptly ends in laughter.

The sun abandoned us
and sent her rays to our graves
along with our hopes.
A sad window
shattered the beams
and blocked out what we wished for,
so we settled instead for
broken needles of light
through wire mesh.

At the circus
a clown was the jailer,
and when his whip had enough of lashing
the naked lion slept.

The naked are drowned in their silence,
defeated,
not a thing any longer belongs to them
but eyes
that try to blinker their nakedness.
Failing,
their tears make a full confession of despair.
Exactly at this moment,
all that seemed indispensable is now useless,
all ambitions cast into a void,
together with stripped-off clothing.
They lie humiliated,
degraded, and beaten.

But tell me please, by the Prophet,
why do the faces still smile,
still keep their word,
sing of resistance,
still make her[11] victory sign
with lifeless hands.

---

11. Egypt is feminine in Arabic.

Halted, thrown to the ground,
knee-deep in blood,
the memories of being beaten
vow to efface themselves.
All who said,
that now history will be written,
a civilization etched in stone,
have failed to comprehend,
have never passed through prison tunnels,
weren't undressed with eyes,
have never slept naked on tiles.
They didn't read the painstaking history
in the lash-lines on our backs.
Not the one in museums with maps and graphs.
All that we learned in school was wrong
all the lessons
wrong,
all the running in all the games we students played,
wrong.
All that we got out of it was
ignorance and foolishness.

When we passed through the schoolyard fence,
we came to the house of injustice.
Our mentors said, "Prison is really
the best place for learning."
And I said, "Lo and behold!"
and the academy of humiliation was prison.
Its classrooms opened their doors to us.
How we loved it and loved our teachers
when they told us tales of the mighty Nile,
of honor and prominence,
even though
they would shear our hair
and would make us wear a smock
that matched an inmate's uniform.
And I was taught that if my buddy ever broke a rule,
he would have to be beaten,
and I would have to rat on him.

Oh school, what class did we drop
from our studies?

You wanted to graduate an honorable Bey?[12]

Rest assured, fear not,

I know your lessons by heart,

but I keep them in my bag for when I need them,

even though I never will

except for retribution by blood.

12. An honorific title used for chieftains or rulers, currently used as a courtesy title in Egypt similar to sir.

KNOWLEDGE

I know,
as one who has tasted pain knows.
My mother's tears were
shed from my own, in fear and yearning,
when I opened up
on fleeting nights we shared.
Our emotions played on the phone,
from my father's frail, trembling voice,
to the simplest words in language,
from philosophy,
to a scar on Mustapha's forehead.
Now the greater part of my knowledge
involves a police station and life behind bars
a bitter bite, dipped in helplessness,
the friends-in-detention,
and bread.
They are crying on the night of Arafah[13]

13. Arafah is the second day of Eid-al-Adha, which is when Muslims around the world perform the Haj pilgrimage.

for happiness caught in the throat
like a bite too big,
for alienation and want
for the first taste of Eid.
Our knowledge grows and grows,
gathers every detail.
We all know 'Ashmāwy,[14]
the police sergeant,
and we know each other well—
our names, our faces,
our stories.
As soon as 'Ashmāwy's door bangs shut,
songs scatter through the night,
words sprinkle across straw mats,
with glasses of tea,
with cigarettes, local and foreign,
with other sorts of smokes,
smuggled in,
I don't know how.

14. A reference to the prison guard who performs executions (capital punishment). This name is given, culturally and historically, to the cruelest guards as well as to executioners.

There is so much hidden
in the details,
caught in the look of a face.
Sheikh Yassin,
you can see, is the oldest among us,
old in years and knowledge,
adept at prison life.
He knows immediately, but moves slowly—
wise, opinionated, and eloquent.
Ahmed El-Ganaynee[15] tends the cellblock.
He isn't expert at cleaning but
excels in prison life[16] and song.
His voice carries to the farthest wards,
and its echo reaches beyond the courtyard.
"Waaaaard!"
Everyone attends
even the steely bars.

15. The last name means gardener.

16. The author uses a contrived word, 'anbara.

We say good evening, flowers and flowerets.[17]
Every man is gallant,
we greet each other for the heck of it.
Oh night, we have no need for a false friend!
I have a friend,
framed for a stash he knew nothing about,
an ammunition box, a rifle, and two cartridges,
even though he was caught with drugs.
And I have a friend who used to
spend the nights mugging commuters
for 50 dollars at gunpoint.
By chance, he accosted someone he knew,
and you know what that man said?
"You look familiar, aren't you Uncle Hilal's son,
Mohamed, I think?
How come you are mugging people on the road?
I didn't know the Hilaliya could breed a thief.
Your father, may God bless his soul, Sheikh Hilal,
has a life that shines like pearls."

17. We say rosy morning/evening a lot as a substitute to good evening, and then we qualify the people around the evening as different flowers, like roses, jasmines . . . It's like saying that people make the evening as beautiful like a garden of flowers.

So my friend said, “Alright, I won’t treat you
like the rest then, just give me half.”
So he paid him half, and for sure,
who you know makes a difference!

Who doesn’t know Alaa Abu Samra?
Everyone behind bars knows
that no one knows him.
Orphaned from a tree, the poor dear,
no home,
no homeland.
He does not belong anywhere
or to anyone,
not in any direction
on Earth.
Every day he gets hold of the smuggled phone
and takes his time,
pacing back and forth,
contracting time and space.
Then, after much drama, “Here you go, bro.
Thank you for your courtesy.
No one is on the line.”

We laugh and then stop all together,
in sync intellectually.
We laugh and cry
for the country,
for the sun that appears and vanishes,
for family, friends, home,
and for the beam of light that was buried,
we cry and read the verses of al-Fatiha[18]
over the grave.
Brothers in God's night and its damnation,
brothers of common experience,
of common oppressive, sad,
and disgusting things.
We know the delusion of knowledge,
if only you knew, it is massive.
But I can still say
that I love, that I dream,
get inspired,
and get hurt.
The booming of the poem
vibrates inside iron bars,

18. The first Surah in the Quran, always read for the deceased and during rituals.

but its wrists have never been shackled,
nor has steel ever muffled its songs,
nor has the voice of an ode become hoarse.
And I am still able to be inspired
and to be hurt,
to love, and dream, and utter,
to write about a prison that
has a dove above its walls.
And I tell my mother in a smuggled call
between us,
it's almost over, Mama.
I draw on Mustafa's forehead
the mourning mark,[19]
and on my face, I draw a smile.
And oh, how much we have learned here
so much,
and we still don't have a clue:
we see and we stay blind.

19. Many of the people Mohsen encountered in prison had scars either because of their criminal activities, or because of police brutality, or lastly because they had inflicted self-harm.

DEPARTURE TIME

At the time of departure,
the smell of the place profuses.
Fragrances lure you to stay
to remember.

Bodies barely escaping from their country,
and countries only souls escape from.

ON THE BURSH AFTER DINNER

Farewell to the prison bars and walls.

Farewell to friends and our nighttime talks,

when the moonlight was divvied up among us.

The moon in the sky — bewildered, lonely, shivering —

chanced upon you all, so you kept him company

and warmed his light with your coat.

Farewell to windows of wire mesh that thwart hands
from escaping —

while the morning dew seeps in to seek your smile.

Farewell to the stranger you will long for.

Farewell to one you loved and missed — even before you left.

When you're out there, living in the light, look up

to see how many stars are missing from the prison's night.

Farewell to your friends and remember, while you might
be outside,

there are people in here who never forget the ones who've left.

Your fellow inmates still gather on the bursh[20] after
dinner — and talk.

They bring you up in conversation,

---

20. Bursh is the Arabic word for the prison-sanctioned bedding rolled out on the floor like mats which are given to inmates.

and your image enlivens the chatter —

But even before we start,

your name is still here in your handwriting

on the wall across from the door

next to all of ours.

We follow the same order, filing from ward to ward

as every door opens, into every absence of

sun in the exercise yard.

We collect and distribute books, with monthly rations
of medicine,

steal moments of happiness like overgrown children,

as if we play hide-and-seek with the guards —

slipping beneath the bedsheet while one passes.

We take risks, give things a try —

the phone wrapped up, smuggled in during visiting hours,

then caught at the last-minute during inspection,

when a guard grazes it by chance.

Farewell to cell phones caught during lights-out,

and to ones caught from carelessness.

Farewell to the Mixed Courts,[21]
where we came together,
glanced at each other as we were brought in,
and died laughing at the judge
and the lawyers.
Farewell to prison walls and cells.
But the end of your ordeal is still in motion.
Your role still needs to be played out —
Still empty handcuffs await the hands of one who hasn't come.
Still the inmate's uniform will hang on the washing line.
Your empty place is unfilled next to me —
and the things you left behind are here,
with memories, if you recall them, like fingerprints
on the walls — greetings to those who've left.
Your fellow prisoners still gather together
on the bursh after dinner — and talk —
so don't forget us.

21. The Mixed Courts of Egypt (Al-MaĐĐkim al-MukhĐaliĐah) a colonial legacy, an autonomous institution administered by European judges, to streamline legal issues between Egyptians and foreigners.

THE DARKNESS INSIDE IS BLEAKER

It was nighttime
so I lit the lamps.
I don't know what transpired
in the darkness out there,
but I suddenly found
the gloom inside more murky
than the shadows of the street.

I had gotten home late that day
after the others split up into groups of three.
There were things unraveling inside me.
I don't know why it was
on this particular night,
but things inside me were darkening
and for them to lift, we had to part.
I had to be late reaching home,
get a stony response after greeting my father,
cry bitterly with no one to hold me
in stolen closeness.

But oh[22] did she really have to die
to make me disbelieve in the world's embrace
and its warm gatherings.[23]
I tell myself that this world in general
disbelieves in her own light.
But double-crossing world,
I was a bright and blazing bulb
extinguished
in your night.
If I ever light again, I will barely
dispel darkness and dejection.
Darkness lives in rooms within me —
and I move into them myself.
My despair can fit into a pouch.
It's there I live.
The poor one wants to sleep curled up
in another's misery.
We hide in each other's pain,
in what can't be soothed away.

22. "Kann shart tebka mayeta yamma" a rhetorical question, the pronoun a reference to someone absent/unknown.

23. Communal gatherings.

We are detached from a world prized by many —
who die clinging to it.

She's always needed
in or out.
She swears that I resemble her within.
Then I swear that I am not coming back,
that I had no faith in the street's creed,
or a religion that proclaims morning won't rise,
that as an individual I disavowed the group,
I believed in reclusiveness.
She tells me that my prison is not walls or gates,
but falsehoods and illusory lights,
that under them people are always
unclear.
My prison isn't cells,
it's creatures, human beings,
all of life — opposing me.
And, seriously, I have never been social.
Each time I love people in bulk,

I end by hating them.
The opposite happens
with one person at a time,
at least it did before I disappeared.

My dreams could still crack the ceiling
until that day I came back late
when no one was waiting for me.
I was sitting alone smoking,
pondering cautiously,
envisioning wildly,
as if I could walk this world
with a candle balanced on my shoulder.
I turned on the lights, but hers remained unlit.
I wished that life would understand me,
I wished it would
give me a chance,
and wait behind me,
while I crouched down
to unlock her handcuffs.

Until that day when her final light
went out,
there was still a glimmer of a flash
within me that remained lit.

THE LIGHT ISN'T SURROUNDED BY GUARDS

I am the son of my father and Uncle Amir,
I am the son of the soil and of the plow,
a sum total in one single heart
flowing into the wounds of the people.
The throes of my agonies are in
the pulse of this land.
I am the son of my father and Uncle Amir
who taught me to be a sculptor,
to sculpt from the darkness of the night
a luminous horse with my chisel.
I am the son of my father and Uncle Amir,
my friend, my companion — a colleague
because he lent me his glasses.
He dissolved me in his sorrows
and warmed me in the circle of his arms
on internment's cold nights.
His gaze was a duvet of love atop the sleepers
and on those sharing
their blankets on the floor.

There is still goodness in this life, he says,
as long as there's charity —
among the poor, for the poor —
enriching both the giver and the receiver.[24]
My son, he says, bitterness is for the past.
There is only what's left.
His sweet laughter reflects on his cheeks.
Hey, you know what, Uncle Amir, my friend?
I am like Egypt in chains, I make pennies
and live on a gulp of air when starved,
when the change is scarce.
When their palms wrung our necks,
and our souls were suffocated by a hundred chokes,
we relaxed and stretched out —
an inch or a handspan in her prison.
Happy and sad by turns like me,
she cries in the muteness of night and together
we laugh when someone asks . . .
with God's grace we get by, we say.

---

24. Almsgiving (Zakat) is one of the pillars of Islam. Muslims believe that giving to others purifies their own wealth, augments its value, and prompts us to recognize that everything we have is a trust from God.

I am like Egypt in chains.
I look like my father in the photo,
with his worries and suffering.
Our hopes walked slowly at first,
but now they've stopped in their tracks.
They see that pain remains as long as there's life on earth.
But we two are different from each other
in our suffering and in its significance.
My father hasn't shed a tear.
He abandons life — when it wrongs him,
and returns to it — when it's fair.
He said, Life upturns or balances the meaning of our existence.
The world is unjust
even when it's fair."
Even if a child holds back a tear,
it's unable to change the lies of this world.
When his laughter vanishes and reappears,
before my eyes can adjust, there it is again,
all at once, like a dawning sun.
He would rise alone,
hum the melody of his moans

to the rhythm of his pain.
His violin strings trilled.
In his love of birds, he was Sufi,
and he echoed its spiritual soliloquies,
but he neither walked nor reposed at night.
On a stairway he danced
between hope and helplessness
didn't waver on the bridge or give up,
he crossed over.
And he inherited my grandfather's stoop,
along with the spirit of a toddler
delighted by his own first steps,
which he would imitate with his cane.
Hey, Amir, prince of princes, I also limp along,
except I glimpse from afar certain traits
of a star or moon, so I've hobbled along on hope,
even hopped on one foot,
but made it all the way to the end.
I never said that turning back would be easier —
my despair sidetracked me, so I'm delayed.
I am in no hurry with you all.

Hey Amir, I'm being patient.
We will sculpt the horse with bells that ring in
the dawn and reverberate with song.
We will still lean on hope and, behind
our moon in a cell, push on.
We will sculpt the mare with feeling,
our heartbeats pounding with life,
despite poverty and want,
mouthfuls scraped from the bowl.
As I pass by each of you
I'll share my smile equally,
my poetry to the people.
Amir, tell my father Fouad[25]
I'll sing and be sure to say: Hey guys,
"Rays of light aren't surrounded by guards."

25. Fouad Haddad, father of all the poets, and the poetic father of the author. The title and the last line allude to the inspiration of his poetry.

FAWZI

By the prophet, forgive me!
I am not a prophet.
I am just a boy.
I still play hopscotch,
bow with deference to my teachers.

I am not like them in patience,
nor like them in affliction.
But since I am said to be
one of today's messengers,
I will perpetuate that lie to the end.

So long as no instrument exists
to measure patience,
I should pass for a patient person.
But in what way am I like you, my friend?
Given that we are bound together
by the same chains,
how do we justify what has passed

with what is to be?
Why is the iron the same
but not the ordeal?
Our hardships are taken by turn,
but the curse is in the sentence.
Why am I closer to life and sustenance
and you, martyrdom?
I don't want to be grim,
but I am not able to be optimistic.
And I was asking, well,
have you any idea if
bars can stand tall
in the face of the prophets?
Moses, the Kalim,[26] would never
have seen a burning torch[27]
if he had been walled-in.
I will leave aside all the confidence

---

26. Kalim is the adjective that defines Moses since he is the only prophet who spoke directly to God.

27. A Quran reference to Surah [27:7] "Remember when Moses said to his family, 'I have spotted a fire. I will either bring you some directions from there, or a burning torch so you may warm yourselves.'"

of those "brothers,"[28]
and naivety,
which is more demanding
than my pessimism.
I will ask you or I will tell you
or better yet — there is no need.
The question is tedious,
so no need.

Instead, I'll pop into your mind
where I might glimpse a rainbow
or a loved one,
or just people you know,
or those you've seen in passing.
I might feel some warmth for a house
on a street I've never been,
a playground, soccer,
you, running, when you were young,
a brawl between you all
over a goal — in or out —

28. A reference to the Muslim Brotherhood.

or cursing a father's name[29] after a score.
A strike that missed your face,
a laugh when you squabbled and reconciled
at the very same moment.
I spot your girlfriend just outside the field,
logging your time.
And she keeps prolonging the hour —
on a cold day, on a hot day.

Running and fleeing at a protest
in a snapshot caught by a friend
tasting of tear gas,
and people making way for you
to revive a comrade
suddenly passed out.
On the left side
of the photo
traitors and truthful people.
In the back,
a throng, seen and unseen.

29. One of the most insulting ways to rile someone up, since the father is the breadwinner/head of the family. To curse him is to offend the entire family..

I can see you when you spot my skepticism,
and the subtext that murmurs,
it's natural to be broken
at some point, who knows?

Do you know I'm by your side
while we walk to exercise
to pace a meter by half a meter
back and forth?
This is while we are inside,
washing dishes, for example,
or at the window, chatting about the day,
or having fun,
or burning rice
we forgot all about
in the pot,
abashed.
We can't hide our calamity,
but time will spare us.
We can make another batch
before night falls.

While mopping the floors,
while you stack the jugs,
and fill the ones you've emptied,
and I empty the ones you've filled,
and we both dry together.
When we lie on our backs on the tiles,
staring at the ceiling's cracks,
at the wall decayed
like the many who came and went.
At times like this,
I want to ask,
How did you spend the day, my friend?
No, I don't mean the role you've been given.
I'm asking about your attention.
Who did you visit in your mind,
and who visited you?
Did despair for a moment betray you
when you offered to help
in the observation room?[30]
I mean when you saw what they looked like?

30. A medical observation room in the prison where Fawzi worked since he had graduated from medical school.

The life receding from their faces
bit by bit and then gone.
Did a strange feeling come over you?
"Well, thank God."
I was checking up on you,
I mean checking up on me.
Not because I share the drama,
my own wounds will heal.

Fawzi, I don't want to be grim,
but I am unable to be optimistic,
and I was asking if, you know,
if you had any idea,
can bars stand tall
in the face of prophets?

Fawzi, please forgive me,
by the prophet.
This steadfast land lies
in trampled shadow.
All those who take after the prophets

double their afflictions,
compound their chances,
and I am not a prisoner
of two sentences,
nor am I a prophet.

THE BEDFELLOWS ARE SLEEPING AND I'M WHISPERING

A chest rises and a chest falls,
the nights are a breathing pipe.
Walking by the wall, spying
on the morning as it rises, inspiring.

In the deafening
silence of the nights,
in the colossal
isolating barrier,
I grappled with question and answer,
like a mute who strives
to interrogate someone sightless.

Oh, what a story,
the story
of my oppression.

I knew by heart some Ayas.[31]
Oh, years of youth, all lost,
where were you when the world preyed on me?

Beside the gravestone and the wall,
eyes are surrounding me,
they bear witness to the oneness of God.[32]
Nights with obdurate dawns.

Standing guard,
without daring to lean,
shoulder to shoulder,
I leaned despite myself
and was struck hard.
My bedfellow,
who was struck harder,
leaned onto me.
Standing guard

31. Ayas (Ayat) is the plural form of Ayah, meaning a verse of the Quran.

32. Shahadah declaration of faith by bearing witness to the oneness of God, recited before death, when one fears death.

without daring to lean,
I leaned despite myself
on those in front
and those behind me.

Oh, what a story,
the story
of my oppression.
I knew by heart some Ayas.
Oh, years of youth, all lost,
where were you when the world preyed on me?

I knew by heart some Ayas.
I said,
Perish the hands of the Father of Flame,
Abu Lahab.[33]
He took the spring of my life,
oh Lord,
he took five golden years
in his jails

33. Play on the wording of the Quranic verse [111-1] "May the hands of Abu Lahab perish, and he himself perish!"

and left me silver coins instead.
Behind this wire mesh, I spent it all,
although I sometimes believed in the illusion,
like a vast sea without end.

Oh, what a story,
the story
of my oppression.
I knew by heart some Ayas.
Oh, years of youth, all lost,
where were you when the world preyed on me?

Why do they say that prison is for real men?
The blue amulet[34] is in safe keeping
with the old charlatan, a woman seer.
She said, "Listen, so you may recover.
You're a delicate, translucent flower,
and life is a jinni that snatches."
She lives over a hill in a willow
and holds a sharp sickle,

---

34. The amulet is intended to ward off evil, similar to the evil eye.

with a sharp scythe that holds
the sickle.
"You are the son of exodus,
the son from afar,
a roving knight on a steed.
A yearning for the past impels you.
By coincidence, there is something blocking your path
on your way to great things.
Something approaches, odd and uncommon,
whether good or evil, I can't tell.
On your way, young man,
it is written,
you will triumph in the arms of defeat,
and fail when triumphant."

The new Don Quixote fights,
now that life has been unreined.[35]

---

35. Reference to an Egyptian proverb leaving the rope loose from Al-Ghareb (ĐlghĐrb), means letting the camel do as it pleases. Al-Ghareb is the name of the area between the neck and the hump of the Camel.

I said, "Yes, yes, Auntie,
your prophecy was on the mark."
When they said, prison is for real men,
I objected and I said,
"No, no, no, prison is for the dead."
How can I sing, break away, and fly
when dogs have cut my wings?
How do I sing, break away, and seek
when the walls close in,
and bodies close in around me?

Oh, what a story,
the story
of my oppression.
I knew by heart some Ayas.
Oh, years of youth, all lost,
where were you when the world preyed on me?

The bedfellows are asleep.
I can hear the darkness
as it circles the street,

on a twisted path,
aimlessly.
It lives in us, and we in it.
The bedfellows are asleep, and I
am awake.
The implacable wall, murmuring,
asks, "Do you hear it or not,
can you touch it or not?"
Behind a curtain, the ugliness of the night,
a burning flame at the end of the alley.[36]
Nature, my brother, is the essence,
the core of our souls, its reflection.

Oh, what a story,
the story
of my oppression.
I knew by heart some Ayas.
Oh, years of youth, all lost,
where were you when the world preyed on me?

---

36. The flame insinuates both hope and unfulfilled desire.

The bedfellows are asleep, and I'm awake,
the bedfellows are asleep, and I see,
the bedfellows are asleep, and I'm afraid,
the bedfellows are asleep, and I hear.

Oh, what a story,
the story
of my oppression.
I knew by heart some Ayas.
Oh, years of youth, all lost,
where were you when the world preyed on me?

THE BLIND

The first one is basra,[37]
the second one must match the first.
The second is grief — its night,
like curtains drawn for all eternity.
The third is protest —
its streets closed utterly.
The fourth is heartbreak —
the dream turned into dead, discarded bodies.
The fifth told me, "Patience will ululate,"[38]
that it's bearable and will pass.
The sixth sang
for the sweet dew-drenched morning
beyond your curtains.

Oh Egypt, draw your sword from the sheath
and face facts.
Your humiliation

---

37. A fishing card game.

38. Ya lally (ÐÐ lÐllÐ) in the original common filler in singing/ humming like tra-la-la.

has turned our steel
into rust.
Silence is now a disease,
and I have the antidote,
while you, Oh Egypt,
remain mute and obstinate.

Roughing us up
while leaving free
the perpetrator.
You trample those
whose bones
have built your entire edifice
and elevate those enriched
by tearing at your wound,
who march in the funeral
of history, broadcasting the death of joy.

While men in their prime
toil.
A group of wage-workers

make their way, from daybreak,
throwing their salute to the sky
and singing to the morning star.
In the palaces of the stars,
we rise at dawn.
Oh Egypt, how the hands[39]
of the laborers
sweat!

Morning is rising.
It waits outside your door, calling to you.
Oh people, dawn is only bright
with you.
Part the curtains
and fling open the windows.

We can't see the sun
through shutters.

---

39. The poet uses builder (banna- bnÐ) and worker ('amel-ÐÐml).

Oh Egypt,
my heart, that has never loved anyone,
conceived in you.
Crave the light
through your full term,
while still a broken captive,
your cord[40] around your wrist.
You don't distinguish
between the voice of truth and deceit.
Oh Egypt, gather your strength[41]
in this pandemonium
and rise up.
From the core of this country,
I am a patriot,
rise up.

---

40. Cord and pregnancy are homonyms in Arabic.

41. The blind singer Sheikh Imam song lyric – very popular, anti-colonial, patriotic song. https://www.youtube.com/watch?v=KYPYZ--8iZg.

My family, my neighbors,
and loyal uncles,
rise.
My identity card is Egyptian
I don't care about the pains of life
if there is a dream
that can overcome them.
If the one who strives for freedom is defeated,
we can learn from that experience.
If their voice is silenced,
the idea will speak instead.
It spreads in the blink of an eye.
In a single moment, it will make the rounds.

Traitors and bastards
can't make off with tomorrow
after fabricating the past to no end.[42]
Look at how many people
they have exterminated,
but never has an idea

---

42. A play on words that rhyme, an insinuation to the popular idiom "kalam fady": balderdash.

been extinguished.
There is no weapon flimsier
than darkness —
than the killer's plot
of silence, fabrication,
lying, deceit.

In the country of the blind,
perception is distorted.
I will chant with all my strength
until vision comes to pass.
My voice can give sight,
and my chant can reveal.

We can't see the sun from our window
if it is shuttered.
In the country of the blind,
the only real blindness is ignorance.

A NIGHT IN HER COMPANY IS BETTER

Oh sweet one who winds a skein,
wind your way around my heart, my love.
I crown you the sovereign of it.
Your fingers are sweet honeydew.
You make a dome of love from a kernel[43]
and the vast sky from a dome.
Oh, how flirtatious you are, oh!

How lovely you are as you bake a kahk,[44]
Egyptian in roots, temperament, and laughter.
I got lost on the way over because of your beauty.
I limp to your door
with attitude.
A pilgrim,
I talk, sing,
and dance —

43. An Arabic proverb which means to make a mountain out of a molehill (ye'mel min elhabba qubba, ĐĐml mn l-Đbt qbt).

44. Kahk is a cookie made especially during Eid al-Fitr after Ramadan.

oriental, samba, mazurka, or dabka.[45]

For every lover in love — a Mecca.

Oh, my darling,

you're the Kabba[46]

I circle,[47]

I turn, run, walk, and stand —

a dervish,

and my heart loves like a Sufi

as you weave me like wool.[48]

Easy

as you come closer,

I fear the eyes

of the outsider.

---

45. Dabke is an Arab dance that combines circle and line dancing and is widely performed at weddings and other joyous occasions.

46. Kaaba also spelled Ka'bah or Kabah is located in Mecca. It is the direction towards which Muslims pray, and around which Hajj is performed.

47. Circumambulation performed by pilgrims during Hajj.

48. Wool and Sufi are the same word in Arabic.

Our Egypt
elevated in the eyes
of young women.
Egyptians,
worship this Egypt
and plead.
From the faces of her daughters,
learn to read and spell.
Egypt appears in their
tanned appeal
and echoes in their slang.
A laugh from them
creates joy,
while you,
with just your smile,
grieve.

Oh sweet one,
an organ resounds in your timbre.
You give your laughter
with affection.
Your silence is seducing,

your speech, sinful.
Your hushes chime
like a poem
in my heart,
and your words warm me.
The morning came and
my heart hadn't slept,
for the night is better
in your presence.

THE PLACEBO

Young man, stretch your legs
just the length of your blanket,[49]
abstain and surrender.
Toy with possibilities,
but don't go too far.
Accept the hand fate dealt you.
By God, the Sultan,[50] the State,
give up.

The world is
just backgammon,
and you are not a player.
Young man,
extend your stride,
as far as it will take you.

---

49. Egyptian proverb meaning to live within your means, literal meaning is to stretch your legs only to the limits of your comforter ('alla ad-lehafak med reglek -ÐI qd IÐÐfk md rjIÐk).

50. Sultan is used by the author to reference the fact that power hasn't changed.

The poor and the kind
have no land to bequeath.
They have only an empty pocket
to pass down.
They have nothing
to hold onto
but the Sayeda,[51]
their daily prayer,
the prophets, saints,
the unseen.[52]
The poor and the kind
aren't led by pipe dreams.
They don't try the lottery,
or learn how dice can be fixed.
They aren't born to be players,
and the world is a complicated game
with peculiar rules.

---

51. Shrine of the descendants of the Prophet (Sayyida Nafisa/Zeinab/Aisha), also used as honorific titles for Saints.

52. Al-Ghaib is an Arabic expression meaning something that is unseen. It is a concept in Islam denoting all that is unknown, unexplainable, including angels, paradise, hell, future events, which only God knows.

The ones who play are deluded,
flops
and losers —
even when they win.

But simply put, they
philosophize disappointment.
The world's a bitch, a player.
Life is a mixed-up puzzle
with no solutions.
Young man, stretch your legs
as far as they can reach.

You're no messenger
with revelation descending,
and the great message.
Theoretically, what does it matter
to live in accord with values,
or insight, or to learn from defeat?

The notion of playing
is meaningless
in principle.
It has nothing to do
with what is right.
It is purely existential.
But how can we live
and be,
how will truth fortify
the blood of the martyr
and to what end?

Dawn is a dream blacked-out
for the prisoner.
But even before electricity
existed in the universe,
the truth was a neon bulb.

What does it matter if
I will
or won't be?
Or that I was part

of a generation
that was revolutionary
but suffered a setback
in the end.
Our generation
wanted
to recast
life and the stuff of it
and the world beyond.

Then, he believed in miracles.
Now, he had no faith
in potential or destinations,
the self, possibilities, hope,
the odds of fiction coming true.

What will striving accomplish
in a generation where all anyone was taught
was regression, passivity, humiliation,
and submission;

superstition, lack of culture, or Sheikh Konifa;[53]
grit, dullness, tears,
and the passion of Jesus.

We suckled, but we suckled hunger
and drank ignorance at school.
We were so hard-up
that we gathered plastic bags
from the streetsweepers
and made a collection of pebbles.
How will truth improve an impotent generation?
What can that generation accomplish,
when its members are dismembered?[54]
When there aren't any backroads
or detours?

---

53. The sheikhs with beards like Konafa (the oriental string-like dessert). The author is mocking these sheikhs. Half-baked scholars was a popular term used during the revolution.

54. The author only writes the first words La hawla, assuming reader will understand reference to, "There is no power and no strength except with Allah." https://en.wikipedia.org/wiki/Hawqala.

The poor and the kind
were wolves originally.
They are the ones who have really
grasped the game.
They don't play a single round
or lose country or lose faith.[55]
They don't ask God
to repeal what is ordained,
nor do they ask for mercy
in the throes of it.
They know nothing but loyalty,
belonging, illusion.
They are the ones who get the placebo.
They do nothing but surrender,
and you still cling to dreams
and throw the dice in backgammon.

55. Mawla is used by the author to mean guardian, one of the attributes of God.

A STRETCH OF TIME

What do we do in prison except count?
We count then we count then we count,
and for every day gone by,
a bit from an iron bar breaks off
never to be welded on.
The iron mesh is never rewoven.
So thank God for time because not a day
that tumbles from the stretch
ever comes back again.
The last bit I saw fall from the wall
was seconds before I got out.

THE END OF THE ROAD

Praise be to God, who granted us,
at the end of the road,
a coffeeshop —
to bring us together
under a white flag.
So we handed off
to our grandchildren
a cursed switchblade
of an inheritance.
Thank God for war novels,
for stories construed
from our past,
and for corpses to chat about
in our last years.

We start a discussion
and drop it

as though it had never begun,
retell the stories
we lived through together,
and others that we didn't.
We count up who, from yesterday's crowd,
was shot dead and who made it through,
lose track of those detained
and the ones snuffed out.
We argue over mistakes in the tally,
and then with the first call to
pardon without reproach,[56]
we forgive one another.
Disappointments circle along
with the hookah and jokes.
We analyze every set-back in history,
ridicule the next generation.
We chew on all that's left of our losses,
apathetically, like gum.

56. Literally a beautiful pardon, which in Islam means a pardon without rebuke.

We showed up here
with the same faces
as in the protests of the past.
Only our wrinkles were different.
The conversation in the coffeeshop
went like this:

"How does the new generation
strike you, brother?"
The leader of the pack replied,
"They're reckless," to which
a rich man added, "unemployed,"
and a sage said, "foolish."
There are patterns that persist
through generations.
They begin with the first chant
and go on until our demise
at the end of the road.

Then someone said,
"He who, in the last round

of gambling, was wiped out
should, to my mind,
have his ruin concealed —
to give him a fresh chance
to lose — I mean win."
There is something to be gained
by the game itself.
This discovery,
in the face of exhaustion,
will ring true, and the pain
of acknowledging it will be keen.
So let each experience it
for themselves — to feel
what our generation felt,
and then after their defeat,
a later generation will
curse them, but they will
sympathize. "Leave
them alone," they will say,
"it's understandable."
Tomorrow we will surrender

the chairs of those

who were devastated.[57]

Some come to the gambling table

with bulging pockets.

They're ones who won

all the pots of the

revolution.

Winning or losing is irrelevant though.

With loss there is something gained,

if you see it from a different slant.

What matters is living in peace,

secure in your beliefs,

loading weapons with loose change

instead of bullets.

Then the errors increase

throughout the room.

All the opinions tilt

In the opposite direction.

---

57. An Arabic expression (al-maghlubeen 'al-amr, ĐlmghlĐbĐn Đl l-amr) meaning helpless or powerless..

There is someone who has kept quiet
until the end. "What do I think?
Which side am I on?
Don't be thrown by my beard.
I'm still young at heart, and being
old is only shameful
if one's ideas are fossils,
and those who have the dreams
of someone in their twenties
are similar to a young man
whose mindset has
aged from experience.
Victory will be upon us
in any race or color,
when its nationality
is nothing but revolution.
Victory will belong to a generation
that binds the two together.
Boys on the road doing justice
to those who first revolted.
The daily prayer in the square

a prostration for the ones
who began the journey —
the old folks blessed
for the burden that they carried.
With the smallest measures
the army of children
will bring victory
and benediction by the elderly.
The ancestors will be given titles
from both the vocabulary
of conflict
and a children's dictionary —
the children who have been holding
Molotov cocktails, spray paints,
and shawls.[58]
Victory begins over there,
beside a cell,
where we hear
the echo of hymns daily,
from a Surah that descended

58. Shawls were used as protection against tear gas during the Egyptian Revolution.

upon a prisoner at night,
followed by a Surah
that descended on the prophet in Mecca"

Silence suddenly reigns.
We begin a pious spell
as if in prayer.
The coffeeshop has become
a sanctuary, struck
by the curse of history,
its legacy weighing on us
more than a mountain would.
The coffeeshop is a mosque
a communing place for boredom.
Our differences bring us together,
but we are joined
by identical supplications
in prayer.
"Thank God for an outcome
disappointing on every level."
Thank God, oh God,

for those who remain
submissive.
Whenever the Square is mentioned,
the ones whose faith has unraveled
had turned against the dream.
Once the most passionate among us,
in the blink of an eye,
they were altered
by a setback.
You alone are aware, oh Lord,
of the secrets of those who despaired
of ever flourishing, and the content
of their dreams.
Thank God for those who sold illusions
and for those who read bluntly
from what was real.
For those who halfway
down the road
knew that arrival
was far more difficult than
could ever be imagined

and yet went on.
For those who yielded
and bent their backs
instructing us with their blood
as we battled
by showing us a way to win
with a laugh
through all the injustice.

Praise be to God who granted us
at the end of the road,
a coffeeshop —
to bring us together
under a white flag,
so that we might unearth
a story worth telling
in our old age.

ACKNOWLEDGMENTS

First I'd like to thank Laertes Press and Nina Kamberos whose enthusiasm, faith, and interest in this collection enabled me to complete it. Her support and friendship throughout this process has been a delightful surprise. I'd like to thank my sister, Iman Elbanhawy, who has always been my backbone throughout my life and who helped me with the initial translation of this collection. I'd also like to thank Fatima ElKalay whose lyrical insights and natural poetic ability allowed me to convey what you read today. Raphael Cohen who provided a meticulous revision. Last but not least, Mohsen Mohamed, I have been enveloped in his words, his friendship, and insights throughout the translation process. To gain a beautiful kind friend and a remarkable soul like him through this translation journey has been a tremendous gift.